A Son
from Sleep

Also by Rachel Hadas

Form, Cycle, Infinity: Landscape Imagery in the Poetry of Robert Frost and George Seferis
Slow Transparency
Starting from Troy

WESLEYAN POETRY

A Son from Sleep

Rachel Hadas

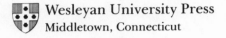 Wesleyan University Press
Middletown, Connecticut

Some of the poems in this book appeared originally in
*Bennington Review, Boulevard, Cumberland Poetry Review, Epoch,
New England Review/Bread Loaf Quarterly, New Republic, Ontario
Review, Ploughshares, PN Review, Southwest Review.* The
quotation from *George Seferis: Collected Poems,* Edmund Keeley
and Philip Sherrard, trans., ed., copyright © 1967 by Princeton
University Press, is reprinted by permission of Princeton
University Press; from Wallace Stevens' "Notes Toward a
Supreme Fiction," *The Collected Poems of Wallace Stevens,*
copyright © 1942 by Wallace Stevens, is reprinted by permission
of Random House, Inc.

Thanks are due to many people in connection with the life from
which these poems somehow grew: my husband, my son, my
mother, my students, and others. I am especially grateful to
Mark Rudman, poet, friend, and neighbor, to whose critical
discernment and uncanny sense of thematic urgency this book
owes its present form.

Library of Congress Cataloging-in-Publication Data

Hadas, Rachel.
    A son from sleep.

∨ (Wesleyan poetry)
    I. Title.   II. Series.
PS3558.A3116S65   1987   811'.54   86-20
ISBN 0-8195-2139-6 (alk. paper)
ISBN 0-8195-1140-4 (pbk.: alk. paper)

All inquiries and permissions requests should be addressed to
the Publisher, Wesleyan University Press, 110 Mt. Vernon Street,
Middletown, Connecticut 06457.

Distributed by Harper & Row Publishers, Keystone Industrial
Park, Scranton, Pennsylvania 18512.

Manufactured in the United States of America

First Edition

WESLEYAN POETRY

To Jonathan

Contents

I

Codex Minor

The headless bird flew back
to the winter root, its tree.
Strong red clay and bones:
stuff my foreign songs
sprang from, not understood
till now, nor now, but hard
against the tongue, the brain—
this late-returning pain
comes surely home to roost.

The village spoke and said:
Your roots are steeped in red,
your bones are benches, mugs,
a shawl, a hut, a tank,
a densely carved-on tree.
Think back to splintered wood.
No name, no family.
The tale not fully grown,
stories not understood.

What does it mean, this late-
night life, ungathered, turning?
Tardy recognitions in the dark?
The blood-red bird flies back to me and says:
Your roots are soaked in red.
I have no song, bird. Make the words for me.
Here is the body; you possess the head.
Escape but find my elemental tree.
Water the roots, blind groper; mouth and spout
beyond all hope of pushing in or out.

The beach in Ormos, then. A single gull
suspended in the air; a porcelain
brilliance; a limpidity; no motion
except Andreas and his son
were working with their hands
in wood. On wood. A boat. A big caïque.
They kissed a little cross
and propped it on the prow
and—gently, slowly—set the thing in motion.
I looked up at the sky again with knowledge.
Could I come here again, I said, to live?
Could I come here again?

Four Fears

Fear in the morning, small, discrete, discreet:
one speck conspicuously tiny in
a field of opposition;
first white hair or cloud against the sun,
momentary, noticed, and then gone.

Night fear, a glowing circle ringed by darkness.
Firelight children cluster
near to hear a tale of outer terror:
Sasquatch shambling over distant mountains,
convicts clanking in chilly woods.

Noon fear, a fiery crumpling of borders,
crackling and flaring, spreading past control,
sucking up force to form a flaming pillar;
centripetal, a ravenous carnation
eating the world and spitting out white heat.

At the hour of fading, fear as no
fire, no color, only deepening absence
so the finale is a yawn or dimple
indenting a bigger or a small black
hole. And no telling where the end begins.

Succession

Usurping divers, one behind or one above another,
are swimming, kicking, rhythmic, deep in murk.
Bubbling, they push, successor on successor,
slow-motion leapfrog dance.
One shoves another down and holds him
in the thick black water.
The frogman son and heir
(down here there is no daughter)
rides on the back of his masked and helmeted
father who thus encumbered
nevertheless is strong enough
to push the old king under
him and hold him down.
Bubbles rise, but everything is silent.
Now through the swaying waterweeds they push
forward. The young rider's hair
is soaked beneath his helmet,
a blond strand plasters his cheek
under the grey glass mask.
The father kicks and starts to swim,
the son rides on the father,
nameless rubble sinks and sifts
to the ocean floor beneath them.
His turn will come:
child on his shoulders, helmeted and suited,
he too will push and push his father down.

Prerequisite

That time across the water:
ground glass, kaleidoscope
spun, made into pictures,
stretched to a disquisition—
impulse of making do with what was given
but also making what was given less,
condensed, transformed, disguised, and so protected.
Foreign, hermetic, brilliant,
a language and a landscape
made mouths at one another in the mirror.

So that the truth lies where?
The answer rises: *drowning,*
immersion, reimmersion.
I found I'd crossed the water
to find that father (lost,
submerged among the living)
whose wartime house site on Rigillis Street
I used to visit, stand at, dawdling, dreaming,
leaning precariously hard
on doomed fragilities.
I never fell. The present
was crumpled up, illegible, askew.
The past was glistening, inaccessible.

Philemon and Baucis

My envy of people my age or older
whose parents both are living
takes the form of contempt.
First, the parents are old.
Old and bald and fat and slow
or old and ill or at the very least
mothers like what their daughters
fear they will become,
or old and well but dull
and rocking on the porches
of wicker-crackling days.
But do the young do better?
Given that privilege, grown up themselves
and looking at what made them in its age,
they fail, they fail of final resolution—
of autumn-gilded clarity, compassion
I am the last to have a right to imagine.
Still, I demand of evening
some slant of light where feeling
is caught like dust motes, floating.
Perhaps the clarifier
is a single pinch of death.

The Cistern

The source is underground.
I put my ear to earth
and hear a hollow sloshing.

It says:
I'm dark. I'm other.
I may be
the truest thing about you
even if, even when
you have forgotten me.
I am what waters your most secret soil.
It says:
I am not angry
but I can no more be
ignored than air or sunlight.
Without me you would turn
first tidily, then hideously dry.
I am the jet of wet,
the drill to the nerve, the thrill
that hits the rocks below the water line.
Or a slow welling up
from a slit to the quick so deep
at first you hardly feel it.

A pause.
Then it says:
Ocean waves lull.
Patterns are pleasurable.
The bearable is what's predictable.
This shape of kindness they
have managed to bestow
upon my living memory in you.
See its ripples.

Hear it bubble.
Child, you ask what pleasure
wobbles in such currents?
Listen again.
Recurrence is a harmless
form of human pleasure.
You have become accustomed to my loss.
Pain furrows lines.
Lines gather into patterns.
I love you. I have wished
you to take joy in process,
the rise and fall
like larger, slower breathing.
There is room for weeping
but weeping is not all.

And my slow answer.
Deep vein,
I hear you. I feel you.
Now that I have found you,
perhaps I will no longer need to trace
your message in each gaze
I happen to encounter.
You know, dark father,
I have scanned strangers,
I have embraced mistakes,
have put my ear to the clash
and knock of many rhythms,
have taken soundings for the sunken figure.
Now the precious phantom gathers truth
out of my own flesh.

The Dream of Severing

Violent, the severing: a son from sleep,
me from my cord, myself, connected to
a head, a body—mine! I wield the knife,
flinch, painless; slice, survive
into new life. Or do I?

And you, the other, cower in a corner
glaring a threat or promise.
I no longer
distinguish these twin poles.
Provoke me, I withdraw;
testing the bond, I scratch it like a sore.

Amnesia, Changes

What was I going to say? I forget.
Chained . . . to cycle?
Let me unbuckle and begin again.

Time—fragrant essence shaken
into the snatched bath.
For fifteen minutes at an essence, then,
to recapture that hoary sovereign the self,
self as she was or as
she seemed to be becoming;
presences; the looming and withdrawing
woman I was and hourly lose, regain

    (bleeding myself, and diapered, I pad in
    to diaper the baby once again;
    my moist hands, soft with ointment like his skin,
    smell like his skin)

—no, metamorphoses are not
yet done, perhaps will never be quite done.
That was the terror, as I now remember,
that I would never, after, be the same.

Up and Down

Days into weeks.
Still night sweats
and bleeding still,
its bleachy smell.
Your bleat softly
shears the thick
fleece of dark.
I wake wet,
cold, hot:
milk and sweat,
nightgown, hair,
humid breasts.
Here you are.
Latch on.
Suck.

Lie down, says the old body.
Get back between the sheets.
Root down, down in dreams.

Your soft call cries no more alternatives.
The bed, the night
make space for three of us.
Silent accommodations in the dark.

Fears of His Smallness

A grain of rice lost in a casserole.

Each daytime's dark demotic
shows me the underbelly,
the flip side, inconspicuous and grim.
The child, a small pale prune-faced flabby thing,
dwindles to broomstick body
or shrinks from cuddly tininess to sheer
invisibility: soot,
dandruff, eyelash, cat hair,
a flake, a merest speck
pinched between thumb and finger,
then flicked out into air and clean forgotten
before it can be shown
the world, shown to the world.

March Light

Through dirty windows
March light whitely
glazes afternoon
pale porcelain,
glazes the bedspread,
glazes the taffy-
colored nest of afghans,
glazes you,
glazes me
singing softly,
old cracked bell
barely crazing
the silence, sweet,
sweet, I keep
wanting to read
to you like verse,
silence to bathe in
clear as water.
I'm learning several
kinds of silence:
flannel silence,
thick, damp, woolly
with infant snoring;
golden silence;
silver silence;
white silence,
whiter than noise,
milky matrix
you inhabit.

In Lieu of a Lullaby

Sleep, sleep, happy sleep,
While o'er thee thy mother weep.

       —BLAKE, "Cradle Song"

What you are sucking is my life till now,
griefs, pleasures, weathers; all the nights and days
distilled, then watered down to drinkable
blandness you unhesitatingly

turn to, take in. My nipples sometimes sting
or ache, are tired of your thirsty tugging,
and sometimes thirst for you.
I fed my own old face until you came.

When you weep it is not yet with real tears.
I do not know your language yet. These bodies
cling together, share a root of life.
And what I weep for isn't broken sleep,

dreamless; or years of broken nights ahead;
it isn't for the broad unanchored wake
of years and seasons and indulgences
that gleams and rolls behind me;

not even that for half a sunlit life
I feared and waited. Not
this, or not only this; whatever might have happened,
it would not have been you

as you are now, here, bumping at my neck,
or cuddling in the corner of the crib.
No. What makes me weep,
awful, automatic as a faucet,

is simply singing you
my pitiful small stock of lullabies.
Hush little baby; Go tell Aunt Rhodie;
Rock-a-bye baby—one and all turn out

to be such litanies of infant loss,
disaster rediscovered, hummed in tunes
that turn my faded memories of babyhood
green and in a twinkling

wet. What isn't wet these days? Tears, blood,
crap, pee, night sweats, dissolving down to new
core, bone to milk: the strangeness, day by day.
You suck this salt

in with the milk, or do you?
Before your birth I feared you'd soak in fears
I croon tonight in words
some other mother once upon a time

made, and other mothers,
loving and fearing, sang, and still are singing:
And if that horse and cart fall down,
You'll still be the sweetest little baby in town.

Late Spring

The cocoon of days swells, stirs,
light lengthens.
But spring keeps on delaying. You and I
are hostages at home of awful weather.
We can't step out into the ankle-deep
slush, you buttoned warm into my coat—
we could, of course, but why?
This time will not come again, you and I
here indoors. The sleet
and roaring wind are hedges,
screens behind which we shelter
alone, we two, all day,
you nestling in the corner of the crib,
damp head hollowing out the pungent lambskin
just where you like to burrow, little vole,
me in the next room writing.
It will be brief.
For once in all my life I'm not impatient.

Lying under a Quilt

Twilight; a drowsy dim
haven of thick repose
and half the journey done,
we sleepily suppose.
Hidden in either self,
memories lodge in lips,
creased into secret cells;
we're quiet, touching hips,

lying under a quilt,
catted on either flank,
our little boy asleep
on the other side of the wall,
and summer still ungroomed,
bugs in the bushy grass,
rain hanging undecided
whether or not to fall.

I see you—shining islands
haloed with sheer desire!
Unearthly mauve and crimson
sculptings of upper air!
I swoop, I solo float,
I sacrifice it all
for color beyond thought,
gesture, ineffable!

Through empyrean brilliance
our son is cast, a shadow
growing up exiled, empty
of what no one but me
or you can give him. You.
You too were left behind!
My arms are empty. Flailing
I thrash, make up my mind,

clip the wide-flung wings
and fall down the bright air
which speaks to me in light:
Come dive me, plunge me, here.
My purifying fire
gilds all you hope to be,
to travel, to discover,
and everything you've done.

           Again my breast
hardens. Milk comes down.
As constant dripping wears away a stone
so I am hard and softened, bottleful
of riches, magical
and always out of reach
till need uncorks me. Gently,
then, the contents leach.

On His Sleep

Each time I check your succulent
    sleep you have once again
done your nocturnal spin,
    completely changed position.
Spread-eagled on your lambskin with one toe
    halfway out the window
or hunched with rump in air are only two
    points of a compass that points everywhere.

Am I a bully, wishing to compress
    your sleep's sweet restlessness
into a smaller area? Nevertheless
    there is this urge to squeeze
malleable matter into little wads
    taking up a minimum of space,
tidy and economic as you please:
    old cars or garbage, readied for new use.

Excretion, birth . . . Or maybe after all
    you are, as infant, equal to a small
but fierce, contentious vehicle.
    Yesterday's headline: *1985*
BABIES HEADED FOR LIFE IN THE FAST LANE.
    Sentence or prophecy?
What did it mean? Was speed supposed to be
    good for those babies? Why?

Lanes. Who are they, anyhow, to pen
    anyone in with broken or unbroken
lines—especially my infant son?
    So soon you will have woken,
have walked, have spoken.
    Think of a bird that's put into a box,
flaps duly gummed and folded and pressed flat
    according to directions: a gift

years later carefully undone reveals
	its contents as a light-boned skeleton;
a pile of feathers decked with beak or claw;
	a moldy smell of staled anticipation . . .
The thing itself, I'm certain, will have flown,
	have left eternal lines (so called) to time
and nothing else behind:
	idea of bird imprinted on the mind.

Plump duckling, each new day like each new food
	you take serenely in, and hungrily
assimilate and make yourself the more.
	What you don't need you easily excrete.
You shake each new day's troubles off your back.
	Desiring you tiny once again,
tucked safely into sleep is only my
	provisioning for what I know I'll lack.

The chubby fist poked out between the bars,
	the foot half numb with sleep,
the mouth half open and its sweet low breath:
	so many separate stars
I want to join together with one line
	and shape an infant constellation
twinkling above the babies in the lane.
	Immortalize you. There's a consolation.

At night your father, you, and I are slung
	in individual hammocks through the black
loom of a jungle restlessly patrolled
	by native roaches, silently. Asleep,
we're each of us enmeshed
	in hours of wordless breath.
Awake, I seem to see us all as shapes
	in darkness, both up close

and also as if from an enormous distance.
   I see we're born to shake the bars, outgrow
the crib, and toddle off—fast lane or slow
   comes to one end. We shake our limbs in love
a little while. Years push us on and on.
   Tired, we are glad to see the cozy pen,
its tidy lines dividing time and space again.
   We climb back in and sleep a lifetime off.

Two and One

Asleep between us
(father, mother
pushing a stroller)
this treasure is.

Gain from loss.
Good-bye, speech;
here in reach
is Paradise

(here in the park,
the dogs, the dirt,
my milky shirt,
cries in the dark)—

was all along?
Yes and no.
Until I had you
I had it wrong.

The focus given—
an infant's face—
they are one place,
Hell and Heaven.

We lose to find.
Youth, beauty,
wave good-bye.
I bend my mind,

strike my temple,
try to grapple
with the riddle,
yet it's simple:

Janus-face,
here you are.
You light up space
like a single star.

On either side
an emptiness—
here Born, there Died—
fills the place

yet fades away
in the glow
of a single day.
I know, I know:

You weren't always here.
And you'll go. (When?)
You'll disappear.
Birth/death: twin

mirrors reflecting
only each other
over the sleeping
head in the stroller

lose their power,
pale in one
brilliant hour
of living sun.

Brush of a wing—
or is it blade?—
flickering
over what we've made,

that angel love,
enormous knife,
wing of a dove
scoring life

swoops its shadow
invisibly
into a meadow
where we three,

mother, father,
baby, lie
close together
under the sky.

Trees are in flower.
Grass is green.
The hour is noon
and is forever.

II

Rhapsody for Thanksgiving

Still another well inside a cave.
It used to be easy for us to draw up idols and ornaments
to please those friends who still remained loyal to us.

The ropes have broken; only the grooves on the well's lip
remind us of our past happiness:
the fingers on the rim, as the poet put it.

—SEFERIS, "Mythistorema"

In a warm room and surfeited with turkey
eight or nine people are sprawling
as if dropped from another planet
though no one comes from farther away
than Worcester, Mass. or France or Yugoslavia.
Into this friendly lassitude the baby
crawls. She is busily weaving
the shroud and loincloth of our kind;
she plaits her fledgling macramé
of consonants and vowels.
Ah, ooh, we say in our several idioms,
reaching out to touch the palm-sized head,
its invisible contents palpably
simmering like an omelet.

In a grocery store in Chinatown this jar
held hundred-year-old eggs;
function that has evolved. The umbrella-stand
phase was its missing link.
It now is a container for potted baby.
She is barely tall enough to stand up in it;
her chin rests on the edge, her dimply fingers
cling to the rim. Snugly
encased (it now resembles a cartouche),
she gazes out, drinks in the polyglot
room where a boy who looks like Le Petit Prince
has begun a Gallic tantrum.

In separate apartments, beds, and bodies
as it gets later, house guests, parents, clerics
digest the day. Turkey turns to us.
Maja in her black nightgown
sleeps a Serbian sleep.
George Bartoks, Brahmses, Mahlers in his mind,
sheets clenched between his teeth to keep the sound in.
I lie and let the contents of my brainpan
balance; stir; let them sink,
like water that fall of drought,
ever so gradually to invisibility:
in wells words fall and echo   stone   dry   stone
a ballpoint pen winks up sardonically
scrawls on the chalk-dry wellbed *tabula rasa.*

In the turkied dark I tell myself
to channel it, remember
the neighborliness and order
in Samos, when the time came round each week or two
    in summer
for moonlit irrigations
of every householder's contiguous kitchen garden.
Lines of tomato plants castled
in little hills of clay;
beans; onions; watermelon;
and the carpophoric water gurgled
quietly on its way
and the irrigation official
raised his hoe, saluting,
passing the water on.

In Santorini, later that same summer,
the seaside excavations:
low Minoan rooms and tall amphorae,
dried black beans by the handful
glittering like disembodied eyes at the bottom
millennia after wine and oil had dried:
peas, lentils, beans deceptively parched and puny
but ready for the slightest moistening.
Add earth, add water, presto!
you had regeneration
locked in the small black germ and now set free.

A thousand years. Two thousand. Near our end,
we keep encoding, scratching deep, engraving
the words and hoping for—what? Some future child
miraculously to plunge
her hand into a crock of brine and pull
eyes, lips wet from the depths,
encapsulated secrets rich as gold.
Baby in jar, seed in amphora,
lies in the mind, music locked in lips,
muses, daughters of memory, teacher, taught,
eater and eaten: these interlocking pairs
lie at the bottom of some deep vessel
musty, lucky, and empty, filled tonight
with possibility and nothing else.

The morning after
all this has been assimilated
more or less easily into each turkey-eater:
Maja takes off black satin and squeezes into English;
George surfaces in words;
I wipe the bits of straw and salt and alphabet
off my dry lips, look out the bedroom window,
see pigeons on the roof of the synagogue.
The cats cluck at them, chatter: truest flattery,
such faithful imitation,
both leitmotif and every day's fresh dreamtongue.

Time in its washing fills and empties vessels,
irons out wrinkles, yawning, a Degas washerwoman;
and the baby bends to her bed of vocables
hoeing careful channels out.

Oh, language: elevator, envelope,
and centrifuge; bed and board;
Chinese jar and puzzle;
warm clay and seedbed;
house a decade back beside the sea:

we sleep and wake and sleep again. The seeds
wait, patient, in their desiccated coats.

That Walk Away as One:
A Marriage Brood

Morning and afternoon are clasped together

And North and South are an intrinsic couple
And sun and rain a plural, like two lovers
That walk away as one in the greenest body.

—WALLACE STEVENS, "Notes Toward a Supreme Fiction"

1

I was never accused of beauty
but nothing is left here but the body
I wrote at twenty-three,
living on a beach where bodies mattered
and married. Sun beat down.
It was a way of saying who I was:
marriage, marriage, not the red-brown body
bewildered by its being on the beach.
It was a shape of time, a path, a way.

Now I have married again
and do not live on a beach.
I work indoors. I live indoors. I teach.
I worry less about beauty
(a good thing, too) and give
less time to flesh and people
say *Married? Somehow you don't*
look married and some snake
bites its tail. I turn to words. I brood.

2

Human time and circumstances; shared
secrets; this face I carry around with me;
privacy's fleshed core, as individual
as DNA, a brow, a bone, a nostril.
You say I don't look married. Who are you?
Compendium of silences and strangeness,
man I know not at all, whose outer shell

I barely recognize, what do you know
about green into gold and stories told
in lamplight, absolutely
illegibly private and absurd? of limbs
tangled in sleep? of—no.
Our flesh almost no matter what
we do in it is secret.
Eyes, cloudy mirrors out of which and into which we peer,
bear smudges, fingerprints; no premonitions
or scars of memory, tug of lip or chin,
time's sculptings, lilt of a voice,
swing of a walk, the sheets from which we've risen—
invisible and anyway profoundly none of your business
except perhaps I partly want to flaunt
these secrets, this open secret known as marriage.

   3

A. describes his cousin's wedding in Woodmere:
the bride revolving on a Lazy Susan
spun slowly into view, then up the aisle
as if on casters; the moment of antic-
ipation clicks its camera, she's done,
laminated into instant memory
flippable to in ten or twenty years.
There is no present. Weddings fight the present.

Contracts and contractions.
Rings, ceremonies, rites.

4

Still brooding. Axial poles of the marriage myth—
seeming, acting, seeing, being. Look:
women and men impaled
in binary opposition,
separated by the great sexless bulk of the globe.
At one end a soft female melted self,
quicksilvery, darting fishlike, lithe, and boyish?
Start again. One side alive with sex,
the other not? No no. How does it fit,
where do I go, what boundaries describe me?
Question asked again, again, again:
one walks right through the all-surrounding fence
striped red and black in bars.
No one gets out of life unscathed by scars.
This sequel to a vision—girlhood spent,
this woman walks in relative
freedom down the street,
abstracted, tired, knowing who she is, a little.

The mother goddess then at one extreme,
a slim young twinkling girl-shape at the other?
I didn't wear an apron or talk about my children.

To see all things from outside, curable,
three-dimensional, palpably reflecting
the way we look to others. Disembodied
bodylets; rounded creatures filling space;
questions rise like blood to the cheeks, the air.

5

I cross the still-wet street, still silvery
one September morning, after rain,
after voting in the primary,
and awnings dump their glistening loads, a flock
of pigeons swoops and scatters
over a grey-gold cloud and again away
as gilded puddles give their radiance up
and sky reflects the mix of doubt and bliss
and dreck and am I married?

6

Not whether we march two by two
but where we march. Not where
but how much time we have left.

7

Locked out of the apartment for two hours
by whom you couldn't figure out, you saw
the whole world differently. The corner of
100th Street became the center
of a chilly nervous circle
glances edged into, scattered off again.
Thresholds, forebodings. My
sprawled body—locked away from light?
Nameless marauders bursting through a window,
trampling down the long dark hall toward—No.
Feeling frail and frozen,
you stuck your cold gloved hands
deeper into your pockets, went on waiting.

And I was coming toward you on the subway,
safe as one is in there, which is to say not safe
at all: alert in a jungle of moving eyes,
threads, voices, breaths, and through quotidian
arcades and possibilities, a thick
silence composed of tiny
chaoses, a labyrinth I daily
negotiated—I was coming home.

Love, love—it's terrible to say this—means surrounding
    walls,
partly means doors, means silence,
means locks. I bury my head in your shoulder,
you take me in your arms—the arms that circle,
hold, and enfold also ward off, keep out.
Even our precious silence is partitioned,
glittering with eyes I shut when I get home
but only at the cost of other golden glimpses.

8

Teaching is talking, and I teach and you teach
and come home in our dunce caps,
mute, sullen, deaf, and blind. Cup. Table. Bed.
What was that you said? I didn't hear you,
you didn't hear me. Vat or cistern, pool or bank—
it's empty. Lately even dreams of speaking
muffle my mouth in wool.
Words, words, words unreeling from the head
onto a clouded blackboard, illegible and lacy,
smudged as soon as scribbled; smoky breath
spiralled up into the evening air,
smoke rings from your pipe. All disappear.

Yet one can find an hour of pure unsaying.
Anesthetized by stillness, I lie down,
mouth and eyes closed. The cat on my back,
solid and pat, a blob of sealing wax,
shuts, perfects, protects me,
and presently a distant vista opens.
An azure eye meanders over a shining sea

years ring with brilliance.
She sits in an open doorway,
hands in her lap, a bowl of uncracked almonds
beside her, fresh and fragrant from the tree.
Idly she gazes to the south.
All morning is before her.
Clear, far, and tiny, in a mote of light,
everything vanishes but pure potential.

I can remember the color of the bowl.
The dim room brims with possibility.

9

What do I care whether or not I (we?)
seem married? Voluptuous idiot,
language is the bridegroom
I roll with in exhaustion
Thursday night, after a week of teaching.
Succulent intentions
sponged from the blackboard, sunken in the head.
Happily enough we swim in the dimness,
blowing our bubbles of words and music.

10

This afternoon I came up the stairs from the subway
at the southwest corner of Broadway and 96th Street
at the exact same moment you were striding
north on that corner. Tall; dark overcoat—
it's false to put together
recalled details, as if I'd seen a stranger.
How then to remember and separate what I saw?
It was you. Pure pleasure in recognition
doesn't say it either. There you were
so simply before my eyes and walking fast
and a split second later you saw me too.
A gift, a gift! Did we kiss? I took your arm,
we hardly missed a beat, we crossed the street
and did our errands—wine, squid, number one
pencils, grapefruit—went home; went on living.

This walking arm in arm in harmony
having come from separate directions—
this is marriage too. It looks so easy
and is perhaps so easy and is not.
It always is a gift.
It gives a form to life
perhaps invisibly. I don't look married.

Little by Little

Let nothing be too big or small to say or see.
End of the world; cockroach on the counter;
déjà vu; tail of a dream; anonymous phone call;
child asleep; kettle begins to boil.
Over the ribbon of winter river creeps the sun.
The pigeon preening on the synagogue wall
ruffles its wings and tucks its head back down.

The daily touch of hands
by gradual degrees turns white to black.
And there are other signs of tender wear.
Cats softly rub their chins on edges they make dingy.
Slow concavities, step by step,
hollow out the hardest granite stair.
Such are the markings I sit down to make.

Secrets

1

The magnum opus when it operates
must have to do with secrets,
their weaving and unravelling, their wall
of hurt archaic smiles and heavy folds
of drapery that barely
stir at processions filing past behind them.

Must tell the secret. Must uncover language
as medium of nothing except mysteries.

Skating along or diving
under. Rhetoric
pumped full and blowsy, drained again, limp, empty:
language to mine, soak, pan the gold, or skim
the surface of. For instance:
I write, we camped, she gave us
fresh vegetables from her garden

List, mood, event, encomium, or question,
and everything's relation to the word.

Babel the half-tamed half-grown cat has new
kittens, a squirming mix from different fathers,
all mewing, all mewed up in one warm tongue.

2

Awake or dreaming, loosely lapped in moonlight,
cargo of each day's secrets.
Staring at the clock face of the moon.
Yesterday, tomorrow
my light thoughts drift and hover

near the sunny window, float
away as clouds do, gently
beyond the bounds of gazing.
Out of reach. My—what's
the phrase?—my train of thought
blown all different ways,
and as with thoughts, so days
spin with relentless speed,
before, before, behind.

How did I manage those few things I wrote?
Did something turn and clasp me like a lover
fiercely in the middle of the night?
Where did I go, stamp passport, and come home
to scribble pages morning would uncover?

3

You love, you irritation, you
untidy room: stay put,
all of you, exactly as you are!
And there is no staying.
And out of the folds of the mind
out of the swamp of summer
out of the dark and light
a place of idleness
and peace, infinite time
leisurely espoused.

4

We live in heaven but we keep forgetting,
fearing a rupture through the garden wall,
terrified the gate
will open, the least crack

gash to wound, consume
the flowered fabric of a flimsy tent.
We live in heaven,
the other side of hell.

5

In the quiet
great patterns
come out like laws
carved on hills,
undug mounds
rich with buried life.
These hot days
I both don't fear
death and fear it
more than ever,
am sad for this last
summer of pauses,
silence, reflection,
sitting still
before the onslaught
of the unknown
and am me
impatient still.
Only let
summer be summer,
place where nothing
is supposed to happen.
Out of the dark
of unshaped dream
words into flesh,
wish to daylight.
Lazily poised,
slowly floating

upside down
in a middle
world where both
poles are true,
inside, outside,
who can know
what is doing,
making, brewing?
Ancient tracks.
Pawprints, dust.
Dead ripe raspberries
hang for picking.

6

The power of language muffled and afraid.
Between friends silences.

Robert Frost sits in a trough
telling truth after truth.

An aviator rescues prisoners
from the interior, flies them boldly home.

Muted, I keep peace,
turn the lights down, open

the door and wander in a long wet park.

7

Terrible, the tentative and slow
creation of the world. Vision. Re-

vision. Color sounds
over the rim of the globe.

Surge of trees. A hill
bursts into being. Pause
and suck for breath: a summons.
A flood like love from nothing into something:
sum of an absence lured
somehow over and over into being,

sighed the magician, picking up his wand.

8

You see? No secrets
told at all.
Only this key.

Gold in the dark!
A russet vein
branches downward:

pylons, arches,
porticoes. Hands
thrust through walls

of brick, touch
finger, thumb,
wrist, arm,

a woman's body
on a blanket
sheathed in sand.

No, two women,
alive, dreaming.
I have dreamed them,

dream you also,
dream a life
made from nothing,

scooped from under
heavy sand,
salt damp flesh.

Now I reach
the water wall.
Fingers fumble

at the hole.

Yes, But

It is irrevocable. Not like marriage
or buying a house or being merely
happy or unhappy.

> Yes, but to come home after some boring concert
> or party, everybody sweating, aging
> and here is this whole other little life
> asleep and floating, waves of possibility

Yes, but it wakes you from the silky or salty
dream-dark you need, you too, your life, your age,
it wakes you with its life   I'M ME   I'M ME

> Yes, but the icons of regeneration
> life stamped deep in the loins and come again
> here and caressable: a miracle

Yes, but the cold prepackaged
duck whose preslit innards
I tugged and scooped this morning
packed in so tight   socked in
the flesh, the cavity, the sealed-in blood

> Yes, but this is backasswards. Birth is not
> through throat or anus, not through eyes or finger

Yes, but it is downward

> Yes, but down, roots, rain, the pull of earth
> making from nothing and they pull it out

Yes, but then the toys strewn over the floor
the magnets stuck to the refrigerator
door that recapitulate our A
BC for Civilization all to be learned again,
Lamarck was wrong, I was born bare of Greek
nasty and brutish   small and ignorant

     Yes, but primary colors dragged with a loaded
     paintbrush over paper rich and dripping
     rich smell of fingerpaints loamlike   edible

Yes, culture, nurture, but the world
is lurching toward its close.
Not simply life, this life: mortality
is true, is sometimes easy:
this world, our precious earth, the only one we live in

     Yes, but all ages gutter, limp, and falter
     children bring hope, they push the darkness back

Not this time, not this twilight.
No Yes, no But, just No: it is the end.
We walk its daily weight so dark upon us
unspeakable   we never speak of it
each little future flickers
doomed precious   it goes on but not forever
not long now   oh not long.

and lights across the river,
a barge passes under a bridge
bearing its black message:
the poetry reading falters
in the darkened amphitheater
sirens scream END   THE END
we scream too, friends together
we put our heads in one another's laps
wailing and waiting

Yes, and we look like mothers turned to children
children to mothers   one another's needs
even in the last hour desperate, human
I do not know the end
the clock hands moving   moving
the child's cry in the night
hushes it for a little

that mortal ticking

About the author

Rachel Hadas, associate professor of English at Rutgers University, Newark, has written two other books of poetry, *Starting from Troy* and *Slow Transparency*, as well as a critical study of Frost and Seferis. She has written a number of book reviews and has translated poems and essays from the Greek. Hadas holds a B.A. in classics from Radcliffe College, an M.A. in poetry from Johns Hopkins University, and a Ph.D. in comparative literature from Princeton University. Her home is in New York City.

About the book

A Son from Sleep was composed in Baskerville by G&S Typesetters of Austin, Texas. It was printed on 60-pound Miami Book paper and bound by Arcata Graphics/Kingsport of Kingsport, Tennessee. Design by Joyce Kachergis Book Design and Production of Bynum, North Carolina.

Wesleyan University Press, 1987